CHANGE YOUR LIFE IN 33 STEPS

Maliki Cottrell

ISBN-13: 9781234567890
ISBN-10: 1477123456

Cover design by: Art Painter
Library of Congress Control Number: 2018675309
Printed in the United States of America

This book is dedicated to first and foremost my Mother Donna Cottrell, My brothers and Sister; Joel, Taisha and Kareem Cottrell. My wife and partner Keynell and My Three Son's Chase, Wells and Citi and the thousands of men and women that are incarcerated physically or mentally. This book was written to inspire, motive and raise self-awareness in any and every individual that reads it. Enjoy!

"In Order to succeed, We must first believe that we can."

NIKOS KAZANTZAKIS

Change your life in 33 Steps

Imprisonment can be mental or physical. This workbook provides a wonderful way to turn your leisure time into productive time. The quick activities in this book will help you become more productive and get the most out of your day and life.

The activities you'll find in this book can be used at any frequency, whether daily or weekly, any time of the day, and at any point in your life to help and inspire you. Through these exercises, you will learn how to achieve a more fruitful and rewarding life and be freed from any mental or physical imprisonment that holds you back.

This workbook is easy to read and use. Simply read the quotes and complete the activities listed below them. There is space for you to write out your thoughts about each topic. It is a great way to relieve stress, change your focus, and be more productive with your time.

Step 1

"My resume is going to be as long as my rap sheet;

I'm going to stay motivated and never let life relax me."

Activity: Start acquiring skills that will make you more marketable (trade, education, etc.). On the lines below, list the skills you plan to acquire and set a deadline to acquire them.

SKILL   **DEADLINE TO ACQUIRE**

Step 2

> *"Bye is all she said when she left me for dead, so angry that my face turned red; 'I'm going to make something out of myself' was all I said in my head."*

Activity: List five things that inspire you to change.

1.____

2.____

3.____

4.____

5.____

Step 3

Many people today consider prison time, time wasted. How can you make the best of your time in prison?

Activity: Select one of the following, and then explain your answer below.

A) Learn a trade
B) Complete Programs: ASAT, ART, etc.
C) Take college courses
D) Exercise
E) All of the above

____

____

____

____

____

____

____

____

____

____

____

____

____

Step 4

"I am open-minded and ready to explore new avenues;

change starts within, not on the avenue."

Activity: Write what this quote means to you in five sentences or more.

____

____

____

____

____

____

____

____

____

____

____

____

____

Step 5

"Side by side are people who share the same pain,

just remember there's always a rainbow after it rains."

Activity: Take a moment and imagine your future. Describe in as much detail as possible, what your ideal day would look like. Where would you wake up? What will you eat for breakfast? What kind of clothes will you be wearing? What would you do throughout the day? Go to the office? Go to the gym? Go shopping? There is no limit to your possibilities; let your creativity run wild.

____

____

____

____

____

____

____

____

____

____

____

____

____

Step 6

"Taking shortcuts and cutting corners, won't get you anywhere faster;

Plan your moves ahead of time like chess masters."

Activity: Write a Plan A, B, and C of what you are going to do upon your release. (Be as detailed as possible. Have a task to do for every hour of your day. Write down what you're going to do at 9a.m., 10 a.m., and so on and so forth. Go over it every night to make sure you are on track.)

PLAN A   **GOALS**   **HOW I WILL ACHIEVE MY GOALS**

Step 7

"It's easy to say what you're going to do, but harder to do it;

success is what you get when you put your mind to it."

Activity: Go over the goals you wrote on the previous pages (Plans A, B, and C) and write down all of the ways that you can start taking steps towards those goals while incarcerated.

Step 8

"A man without a plan, is like an elephant in quick sand."

Activity: Make a to-do list for today of five to ten things you need and want to get done today. (Examples: 100 push-ups, read one chapter of a book, write a letter to a loved one and thank them for supporting you, etc.)

Step 9

"It makes me feel good, it makes me feel sad,

I am going to stop filtering and looking at the bad."

Life is all about perspective. You can look at everything "negative" that happens to you and find the good in it. Life is 10% what happens to you and 90% how you react to it.

Activity: Write down a "bad" thing that happened to you, and then list all the good things that can come from it. Example: you were sentenced to do prison time (bad). Being sentenced allowed you to clear your mind, reflect on what you can do better, and made you an overall better person (Good!).

BAD THING   **GOOD THINGS THAT CAN COME FROM IT**

____

____

____

____

____

____

____

____

____

____

____

____

BAD THING	**GOOD THINGS THAT CAN COME FROM IT**

Step 10

> *"Life is like playing a game of cards with a set deck;*
>
> *even though you'll win, you won't get respect."*

Activity: Write a paragraph about a situation in which you regret taking a shortcut. Explain why the shortcut wasn't worth taking.

Step 11

"Day in, day out, I take the same route. Today I am going to speak with my actions, instead of my mouth."

Activity: Starting today, stop saying what you are going to do and just do it. Actions speak louder than words. A wise man once told me to keep my plans to myself because if the devil hears you, he will place as many obstacles and temptations as he can in your way.

Step 12

"*What is rich? What is poor? I'll find out when they open that door.*"

Activity: Write your definitions of rich, poor, and success.

Step 13

"It's not what you do, it's how you do; do what's best for you."

Activity: Make a list of your strengths and weaknesses, and for each write an example of actions that you can take to improve each strength and weakness listed. Promise yourself that you will do the right thing once released and promise yourself that you will not let criticism deter you from doing what's best for you.

STRENGTHS   *ACTIONS TO IMPROVE*

WEAKNESSES   **ACTIONS TO IMPROVE**

Step 14

"All is I need is a shot and I'll make it to the top.

Stay patient and opportunity will knock."

Activity: Make a list of a minimum of five people that you can talk to whenever you feel tempted to do the wrong thing. Add as many people to the list as possible. (This becomes your support group.)

____

____

____

____

____

____

____

____

____

____

____

____

____

Step 15

"I once was true to the game, but now I am true to myself.

I can stand on my own, but I am not afraid to ask for help."

Activity: List five things that you need help with. Then list five people that may be able to help you with those problems, then reach out to them. "You miss 100% of the shots that you don't take, shoot your shot." If they are unable to solve your problem, keep searching for other solutions. The answer may be right in front of you.

THINGS I NEED HELP WITH   **PEOPLE WHO CAN HELP ME**

Step 16

"Life is only as hard as you make it; stay focused and don't give up.

Think Bigger! Grow Bigger!"

Activity: List five ways that life can get harder, if you continue to make bad decisions.

____

____

____

____

____

____

____

____

____

____

____

____

Step 17

"A downward spiral was once the direction of my life,

now it's time to be productive so things can go right."

Activity: Do one good deed today. The deed doesn't have to be big, expensive, or even acknowledged by the receiving party. Just do one good deed. Example: give someone a compliment, make a donation to someone less fortunate, etc. Describe the good deed below, after the deed is completed.

GOOD DEEDS

Step 18

"I was born to win, and refuse to lose; I am going to make sure

I succeed and stop crying the blues."

Activity: Write a list of all the people who made something of themselves that were once in your situation or worse. Look at it whenever you start to doubt yourself.

Step 19

"I can feel it, I can taste it; my incarceration won't be time wasted."

Activity: Write 5 examples of things people do in prison that are a waste of time. Write 10 examples of things people do that are not physically incarcerated that are a waste of time.

Step 20

"I am what I make myself. I am a reflection of my choices. Take life one step at a time; these activities are not pointless."

Activity: Write down one lesson that you learned from this book so far and how it has helped you. Then recommend this book to a friend, associate, colleague, or family member.

Step 21

"Being open-minded is the first step towards success. When it's your time to shine, you will leave a lasting impression that the world won't forget."

Activity: Start looking at your future self from a global perspective, not a local perspective. Don't make decisions based on what is accepted and the norm in your neighborhood. Start implementing habits and practices that have been proven over time to lead to success. For example, the average millionaire has seven streams of income so if you want to be a millionaire you should work on having seven streams of income.

Write down three habits or practices that have been proven to lead to success that you will add to your life.

Step 22

"I promise to take advantage of my resources and opportunities,

for it was my lack of creativity and bad choices that ruined me."

Activity: Write an example of a time that you thought you couldn't do something because you lacked the resources, and then describe how your creativity helped you accomplish the task anyway.

____

____

____

____

____

____

____

____

____

____

____

____

____

____

Step 23

"Life is just passing me by; sometimes I daydream and just look up in the sky. I ask myself, 'Why do I continue to live a lie,' then I snap back into reality because real men don't cry."

Activity: Take 10-20 minutes out of your schedule, sit alone, and think of all of the positive things you plan to do upon your release. Write a list of 10-20 positive things you will do once you are released.

Step 24

"Other people have determined my fate;

but it is I who put my life at stake."

Activity: List ten ways that the choices you make today can positively affect your future.

____

____

____

____

____

____

____

____

____

____

____

____

____

____

____

Step 25

"Money, money, money is all that is on my mind. I have to stop worrying about that and continue to free my mind."

Activity: Don't stress about the future too much. Focus more on the present and the moves you can make today. Write one thing, one goal, that you can accomplish today that will put you one step closer to your bigger goals.

____

____

____

____

____

____

____

____

____

____

____

____

____

____

____

Step 26

"What can I do? What should I do? The choice is up to you!"

Activity: On the following pages, make a schedule for yourself. Organize your day, leave little to no time for stress or idle time. Get busy.

DATE	**TIME**	**ACTIVITY**

DATE   *TIME*   *ACTIVITY*

Step 27

"I feel like I'm losing myself. I feel like I've been hit below the belt. Everyone gave up on me, but I won't give up on myself."

Activity: Make a list of all the people who have written you off, given up on you, or left you for dead. Make a name for this list, and every time that you feel like giving up or not giving 110%, take a look at this list. Use them as ammunition to achieve your goals.

____

____

____

____

____

____

____

____

____

____

____

____

____

____

Step 28

"Give me a little and I'll turn it into a lot; it's ambition that separates the haves from the have nots."

Activity: Write a list of three people who started from the bottom and are now at the top. Select one that you would like to be just like. Look at them as a role model and as a guide, sort of like a navigation system. Follow the steps they made, learn as much as you can about them, and use what you learned about them along your journey. If you do not have someone at the moment that you can consider a role model, make a list of characteristics that your ideal role model will have. For example, "he dresses nice," "he takes care of his family," "he's successful," "he's rich," and so on and so forth.

Step 29

"I know what I am going to do. I know how I am going to do it;

all I have to do is stick to my plan and get to it."

Activity: Make a list of your priorities and put them in the order of importance. For example, you can put "stay free" as your #1 priority, "complete parole without any violations" as your second priority, and so on and so forth.

PRIORITIES IN ORDER OF IMPORTANCE

Step 30

"Change your circle into squares and wherever you want to be,

you'll be there."

Activity: Surround yourself with positive people who are doing positive and productive things with their time. Make a list of people to stay away from and a list of people to get closer with.

PEOPLE TO STAY AWAY FROM

____

____

____

____

____

____

____

PEOPLE TO GET CLOSER TO

____

____

____

____

____

____

____

____

____

Step 31

"I should be sitting at home, instead of a cell;

I believe in myself so I know I will do well."

Activity: Take a real good look at your present situation, and then ask yourself "Do I really want to continue to live like this?" Write a list of things you hate about your present living situation, or anything else in your life, and then write one way of how you are going to change and have a better future.

THINGS I HATE RIGHT NOW   **HOW I CAN CHANGE IT**

Step 32

Activity: Practice relieving negative energy with this breathing exercise. Go to a private space away from people maybe the bathroom stall or your cell. Close your eyes and focus on your breathing. Take five deep breaths and while your inhaling count how many second it takes you to fully inhale and as your exhale count the seconds as well do this five times or for 5-7 minutes when you are done you will feel much better and relieved you can do this once a day as an exercise or meditation.

Step 33

"It's hard to trust anyone, even myself.

Success is going to make up for all the pain I have felt."

Activity: Whenever you feel depressed, think of where you're going to be once you achieve your goals (pleasant imagery). Write a list of 3 painful moments that you don't ever want to experience again, and then list how you got through them. You are a warrior. This is to remind you that you can get through anything. Just take it one day at a time.

PAINFUL MOMENTS   **HOW I GOT THROUGH IT**
____

____

____

____

____

____

____

____

____

____

____

Congratulations!

You have completed the workbook. You are well on your way to success. Keep this book with you along your journey so you can stay focused and stay on track. You have completed all 33 steps.

Recommended Reads

These books helped me along my journey and I recommend that you read them all. These books will teach you about Money, Business, Real Estate, and Life. You can purchase these books on Amazon or at your local bookstore.

#1 Rich Dad Poor Dad: Robert T. Kiyosaki

#2 Think and Grow Rich: Napoleon Hill

#3 The Richest Man in Babylon: George S. Clason

#4 The Millionaire Next Door: Thomas J. Stanley

#5 From Madison Avenue to Rikers Island: Mark L. Goldsmith

#6 A Second Chance: Catherine Hoke

Helpful Resources

Legal Help - Avvo.com: Is a website that your family can go to for help finding a lawyer. Simply go to the website, select the state you would like to find a lawyer in, and enter the area of practice (criminal defense, appeal, personal injury, etc.). You will be able to see the lawyers that are available, their reviews, the percentage of cases they won and loss, their years of experience, contact information, and much more. With this information, instead of just going by word of mouth, or using any random lawyer that you stumble upon, you can compare lawyers and make a decision based on the facts, the years of experience, area of practice, percentage of cases won, and reviews. This website is extremely helpful.

Non-Profit Organizations: When you are released, you can reach out to these non-profit organizations to get help with finding Housing, Employment, Substance Abuse Counseling, and Anger Management Counseling. They may also assist you with getting Health Insurance, and enrolling in Trade School, a G.E.D. program, or College. They update their services all the time, so simply give them a call, email them, or visit their location to get the help you need.

#1 Unincarcerate America: www.unincarcerateamerica.org

#2 University of The Streets: www.universityofthestreets.net

#3 Getting Out and Staying Out: www.gosonyc.org

#4 The Fortune Society: www.fortunesociety.org

#5 Defy Ventures: www.defyventures.org

#6 Samaritan Daytop Village: www.samaritanvillage.org

Certificates of Relief

Because of felony and certain misdemeanor convictions, you may be prohibited by law from engaging in certain types of employment and from applying for certain types of licenses. These disabilities may continue even after you have completed the sentence imposed by the court. If you would like to restore your rights, get a Certificate of Relief from Disabilities or a Certificate of Good Conduct. These certificates will remove the mandatory bar that the felony or misdemeanor has placed on you. You may use them to obtain a gun license, Real Estate Broker license, liquor license, and the list goes on. Having one of these certificates will give you a second chance at life.

- If you have completed your sentence, you may apply directly to the Certificate Review Unit for Certificates of Relief or Good Conduct. If you were convicted in another state or by a federal court, you may apply directly upon release from custody to the Certificate Review Unit.

- By law, individuals who are eligible for a Certificate of Relief have not been convicted of more than one felony. For this purpose, two or more felony convictions stemming from the same indictment count as one felony. Two or more convictions stemming from two or more separate indictments filed in the same court, prior to conviction under any of them, also count as one felony. The Parole Board may also issue a Certificate of Relief to eligible offenders who have been convicted in another jurisdiction but who now live in New York State. A Certificate of Relief may be issued upon an eligible individual's release from a correctional facility or at any time thereafter.

- In contrast to the Certificate of Relief, you are eligible for the Certificate of Good Conduct even if you have been convicted of more than one felony. However, you do not become eligible for a Certificate of Good Conduct until a minimum period of time has elapsed from the date of your unrevoked release from custody by parole or from the date your sentence ended.

- In cases in which the most serious conviction is a misdemeanor, there must be at least one year of satisfactory community adjustment before a Certificate of Good Conduct can be considered. In cases in which the most serious conviction is a C, D, or E felony, you must wait at least three years. In cases in which the most serious conviction is an A or B felony, you must wait at least five years.

- If you have been convicted of a felony, you lose the right to vote. This right is automatically restored when you complete your maximum sentence or are discharged by the Board of Parole. If you have been issued a Certificate of Relief from Disabilities or a Certificate of Good Conduct while on parole, you may register to vote.

- Article 23 of the Corrections Law deals with Certificates of Relief from Disabilities and Certificates of Good Conduct. Article 23A of the Corrections Law deals with licenses and employment of persons convicted of criminal offenses. Consult your parole officer about specific questions you may have.

To learn more and to apply, visit this website:
https://doccs.ny.gov/certificate-relief-good-conduct-restoration-rights

To learn more about me, the author, please watch my documentary on YouTube. Simply go to YouTube and type in "Maliki Cottrell Pioneer Documentary."

You may also follow me on social media at any of the following:

Facebook: Maliki Cottrell

Instagram: @Young_____Stunna_____ (Four underscores after each word)

LinkedIn: Maliki Cottrell

YouTube: Maliki Cottrell